WORDS ARE NOT ENOUGH

WORDS ARE NOT ENOUGH

(a collection of poems)

KELECHI IHEANACHOR

WORDS
RHYMES &
RHYTHM

For information about permission to reproduce selections from this book, write to info@wrr.ng

National Library of Nigeria Cataloguing-in-Publication Data

Printed and Published in Nigeria by:

Words Rhymes & Rhythm Limited

Suite C309, Global Plaza Plot 366, Obafemi Awolowo Way, Jabi District, Abuja, Nigeria.

08169027757, 08060109295

www.wrr.ng

DEDICATION

Dedicated to the unconditional love, selflessness,
determination and strength of my mother,
Rosemary.

ACKNOWLEDGEMENTS

My wife Lynda, whose love and encouragement bring out the best in me.

My boys, Kambi and Kamto, with whom everyday is an adventure.

CONTENTS

VANITY

"Nothing makes one so vain as being told that one is a sinner"

- *Oscar Wilde*

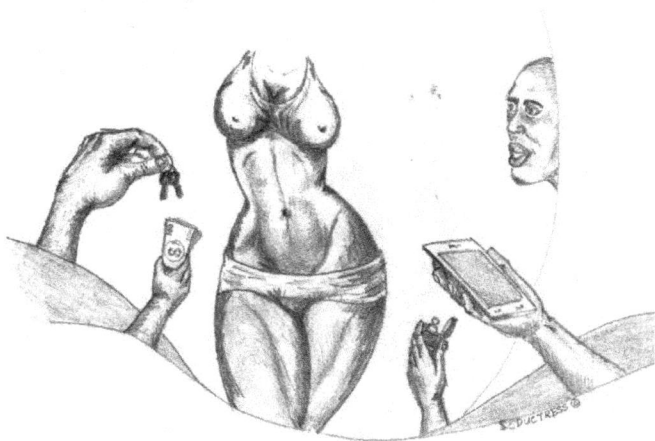

SEDUCTRESS

Clad ever so classy
Moves, smooth and sassy
Her gestures are flirtatious
A smile so contagious
Beguiling wiles of a temptress
Enthralling allure of an enchantress
In decadence she thrives
Of men, she makes knaves

Her lips, thin
Irresistibly tempting
Her ways, perverse
Her touch, so intense
Her mannerism, licentious
Her velvety skin, soft and sensuous
Her gait, pleasing
Constantly teasing

Buttocks perfectly rotund
Hips callously protrude
Breasts in defiance of gravity
Slender legs trot in calamity
Her body, an uneven landscape
Hills and valleys whence no escape
Seduction is her coin
Causing a stirring in men's loins

Consumed by lust
To betray love's trust
Under the hypnosis of a siren's song
For her embrace men long

Passion fuelled by desire
She alone can quench the fire
An iniquitous transaction
Souls of men in barter for sexual gratification

CHILDREN OF THE NIGHT

In paradox with the living world
Day breaks at dusk
Reminiscences of the preceding night
Lost to substance abuse induced amnesia
Breakfast is served
Ecstacy, codeine and cannabis
A balanced diet of solid, liquid and gas
Like a decaying carcass
The remnant of the prior nights hunt
Lays naked and lifeless
Inebriated by debauchery
Only awakened to gain her recompense
Her departure leaves both souls in depletion
Like an eloquent and articulate preacher
The tube propagates hells propaganda
Corrupting the subconscious
By its message of profligacy
As darkness encompasses the metropolis
 Its offspring emerge from the shadows,
Adorned in gold and glitter
Bathed in fragrant perfume
Concealing rot and decay
Congregating in tabernacles of immorality
Flickering and flashing lights
Tobacco burnt as offering
Its smoke rising as repugnant incense
Alcohol and drugs served as unholy communion
Bodies swaying to hypnotic melodies
All in total adulation
To the lord of the night
In this realm of perversion

Where virtue is sacrilege
Abomination is sacrosanct
In pairs they fellowship
Sons with sons
Sons with daughters
Daughters with daughters
To consummate their worship
By sacrifice on the altar of iniquity
In total defilement of their temples
As dawn approaches
The darkness recedes
Only to resurface
At the break of dusk

HOW CAN PERMANENCE BE UNDONE

How can permanence be undone?
Of what gain is an exercise in futility?
Choice is nothing but predetermined outcomes
None is right, neither is wrong
Time and chance or preparedness meets opportunity

Virtue is cold and lifeless
The pleasures of vice bring death
To what end do i strive?
What propels me?
The fear of God or the love of man?

Resentment festering like an infected wound
The falseness of my thoughts
Contaminating my very essence
So I shed my soul like old skin
Leaving behind the guilt and consequence

VOYAGE

"The voyage of discovery is not in seeking new landscapes but in having new eyes"

- *Marcel Proust*

CHARADE PARADE

Hate begets hate
Fatality it's sure fate
The belly of the sated
Churned by hatred
The lame marching in defiance
Gossips in one alliance
The mute raise their voices in harmony
As partakers in the ceremony
Eavesdropping was the pastime of the deaf
Whistling amused the children with lip and palate
cleft
The blind bystanders look in awe
Stunned by the things they saw
Acid bath victim ignored by the law
Hides behind layers of make up in an effort to
conceal her flaw
Nuns soliciting on the avenues
Parading as women of easy virtue
Best friends maintain strangle holds on each other's
throats
While arch enemies raise glasses to toast
Sterile men make a show of their genitalia
Putting post menopausal octogenarians in lustful
hysteria
Making boast of their sexual prowess while puffed
up with self importance
Despite their impotence

3 DIMENSIONS

In company
Amidst friends cum acquaintances
Conversations of barrenness
Chattering lips uttering programmed responses
Smiling faces concealing bitter hearts
Prejudiced minds feigning solidarity
Rancour concealed in laughter
Grudges obscured by affability
Sprained facial muscles
From prolonged smiles of pretence
Ensconced in mistrust
I dialogue with dexterity

In solitude
Day dreams of grandeur
Perfectly orated monologues
Command performances in a one man theatrical
Unedifying thoughts
Instigating self gratification
Memories of unconditional love
Haunting visions of love's lifeless form
Tears shed in silence
Muffled sighs of sorrow
Heart mourns with every beat
Soul grieves till ethereal reunion

In slumber
Dead to the world
Spirit takes flight
To dimensions of alternate realities
On a voyage of discovery

Passage to supernatural realms
Moments of inexplicable clairvoyance
Revelations of the future
Nightmares from the past
Intermittent bouts of cauchemar
Evaded melange with a succubus
Preserved by divine intervention

TIME TRAVEL

The time is tomorrow
Today is long gone
Yesterday was the future in retrospect
Memories are predictions
Of things done yet to come
Where death precedes birth
And resurrection comes before demise
The beginning determined by the end
It only really starts when we all stop
Where or when become irrelevant
Only who and why matter

CHASM

"There is no scarier chasm of darkness than the human mind"

- *Rosanne Barr*

ENNUI

Awakened by the melancholic melody of necessity
Roused by contractual obligation
Against darkness in endless adversity
Evolved into a specie with night vision
Subconsciously performed ritual dances
Penance to restore consciousness
Dispelling transient nocturnal trances
Ubiquitous ambitions of emptiness

Following in the procession of drones
An unwitting conscript to mammon's army
Incensed by the incessancy of ring tones
Pacified by the promise of a debt slashed salary
Obsequious to every instruction
Uttered in hushed tone
Whispered curses of eternal damnation
Fleeting, this heart of stone

Transitory downing of tools
Heralds an ignominious symphony
Renditions by a choir of fools
A ballad orchestrated in cacophony
A holy nation in impermanent delirium
Duality of priests in a diabolical race
Admittance to utility deprived asylum
To find respite in love's embrace

Upon celestial demise
Bemoans a rude awakening
Cloaked in ignorant disguise

A day closer to final reckoning
At every journeys destination
Futile lies all gain
In utmost apprehension
Awakened, again

UNFORSAKEN

A lone wanderer
Trudging through the mind's tundra
Propelled yet impeded by inertia
Frostbit limbs gangrenous from hypothermia
Numbness of emotions
Crystallised blood hampering swift motions
Bones draped in skin
Flesh and imagination stripped thin

A vagrant mind having no destination
Faint from spiritual dehydration
Staggers through life's desert
With no will left to exert
Totters over tribulation's sand dunes
No distant sounds of rhythmic tunes
Tumbling down the steep slope
Tired muscles and diminished hope

VACUA

My minds throat is parched
An unquenchable thirst
Not from lack of water
A glass of ice cold water should suffice
Instead I cringe from brain freeze
I hunger, belly still aching from gluttonous gorging
A futile effort at satisfaction
Another pointless attempt to fill the void
A vacuum not particular to me
But characteristic of all mankind
A gaping black hole
Consuming all in its path
Arts, music, sports
Videogames, television, the internet
Education, work, religion, politics
Alcohol, cigarettes, drugs
Sex, money and power
Temporary avenues of escapism
One can be drunken by power
A licentious beast sated by sexual immorality
Reveling in moral decadence
Luxuriating in the opulence of material gain
Still the emptiness would persist
In the picturesque landscape of personal
aggrandizement
Lies a chasm of despair
Shrouded by superficial calm and collectiveness
Eruptions of a mental volcano
A psychological hurricane of cataclysmic
proportions
The infinite quest for satisfaction

Likened to rainfall in the desert
A sunny day in Antarctica
Insulin shots for diabetics
Poverty alleviation schemes in an underdeveloped
country
All pacifiers in the suckling mouth of an infant
What is this longing that eats away at the heart?
This insatiable craving that brings to naught the
pleasures of life
And to the length of days, tedium
This desire transcends the natural
The spirit yearns to be nourished
Nourishment gotten only from the bread of life
Thirst quenchable only by living water

REBIRTH

"A human being must be born twice. Once from his mother and again from his own body and his own existence"

- *Sultan Walad*

WE ARE WHO WE ARE ©

WE ARE WHO WE ARE

We are who we are
We strive to become who we want
Oblivious of who we ought
Tomorrow scripted by today's choices
Choices made in ignorance
Sometimes right other times disastrous
Steps of faith detour to hell's highway
Encountering salvation whilst on the path of
destruction
The sinner is conscious of pleasure
The saint delights in abstinence
The felon secures his abode
The honest are vulnerable to strong men
The flames of the promiscuous burn bright
The marble altars of the chaste are stone cold

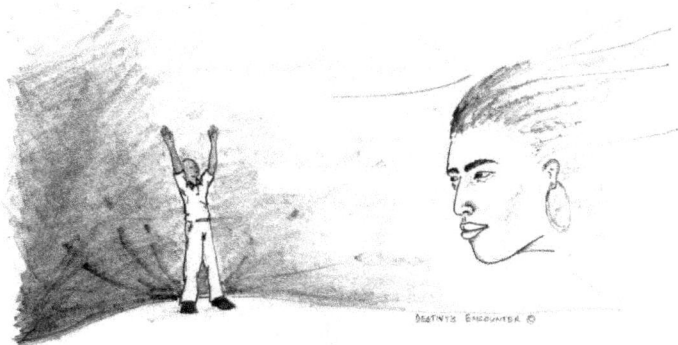

DESTINY'S ENCOUNTER ©

DESTINY'S ENCOUNTER

In my heart a tempest raged
A volatile concoction of extreme emotions
A cocktail of faith, anger, hope, unfulfilment
Of optimism and great expectation, angst and
uncertainty
I sipped with bated breath
Its taste was cold and rancid
Duplicity kept me battling against self
Waging an unending war to subdue my alter-ego
With each battle lost my character was diminished
With every victory my resolve was strengthened
Futility in existence
There has to be more

Destiny comes calling
Her voice is refreshing
Her words, reassuring
My storm is calmed
My spirit, lifted
My soul, replenished
She speaks of purpose
She encourages, inspires
She nurtures my dreams
Fuels my ambitions
Erodes my inhibitions
In her bosom, virtue resides
From her womb nations will be birthed
From her breasts they will suckle
From her essence flows springs of water
My doubts are doused
Extinguished are the raging infernos of my fears

She takes my hand
Leads me out of the darkness of obscurity
Into the marvellous light
She pulls me away from the precipice of death
I am reborn

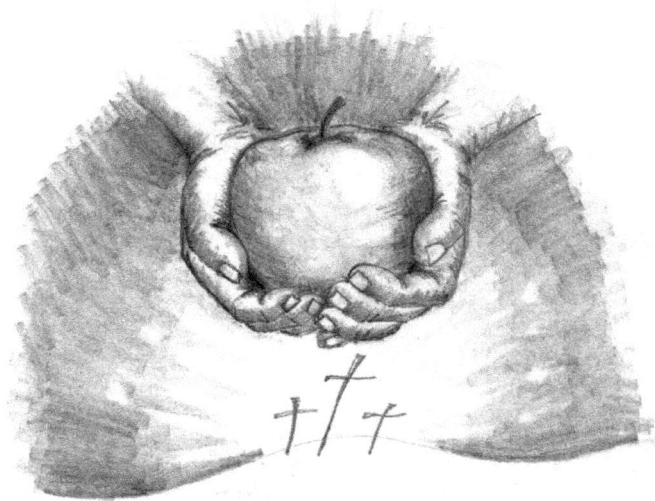

REDEMPTION

The desecration of purity
Omen of the desolation of paradise
Established by iniquity
Sanction for death to arise
Dethronement of the first
Coronation of the morning star
Genesis of the thirst
Enslaved to a depraved master

In tumult and toil
Unending strife in strive
To gain the yield of the soil
Death alone brings reprieve
Upon man and his progeny
A curse of eternal servitude
To the perverter of destiny
Powerless despite divine similitude

Gabriel's Annunciation
Fulfilment of messianic prophesy
Virgin birth by divine conception
In an age of great apostasy
Reestablishment of son ship
Reordination into priesthood
Reinstatement of kingship
Redemption hung on a cross of wood

GOOD INTENTIONS

"Intentions are nice, but ultimately intentions don't really matter because they only exist inside you."

- *Kelly Williams Brown*

DILEMMA

The dilemma of decisions
Torn betwixt sentimentality and objectivity
A humane demeanour whilst horns locked with
adversity
Criticism diluted with kindness
Justice tempered with mercy
Verdicts pronounced on truth as against fact
Judgements made from emotion rather than intellect
Thoughts initiated from the heart not the brain
Profits measured by fulfilment not figures
Smiles accepted as legal tender
Responsibility overshadowing duty
Negative bank balances coexisting with positive
outlooks
Sustained by intangible gains
Rules and regulations non-existent
Laws and decrees abolished
Constitutions rescinded
Order maintained by one command
Decisions reached by one consideration
Love

BLACK GOLD ©

BLACK GOLD

A land once lush and green
Virile and fertile
Fattened reserves from dignified labour
Then the discovery
Greed rears its grotesque head
In its entourage
Nepotism, marginalisation, bribery and corruption
A deprived populace in lack of leadership
Restive youth clamouring for direction
Rumpus instigated by mortification
Balls of fire rage day and night
Illuminating the sky
Ripping holes in the stratosphere
Rain clouds brood in eagerness
To drench the land with acid
Sun blazing with vehemence
Scorching all life
Floating carcasses in blackened rivers
Sullied soil rendering no harvest
In decimation lie the herds of the field
Mother nature drowned
In her own bodily fluids
Life turns to death
Lush and green becomes dust and ash
Peace and tranquillity evades
In its stead
Ruckus and chagrin
Swollen earth
Sated by the blood of innocents

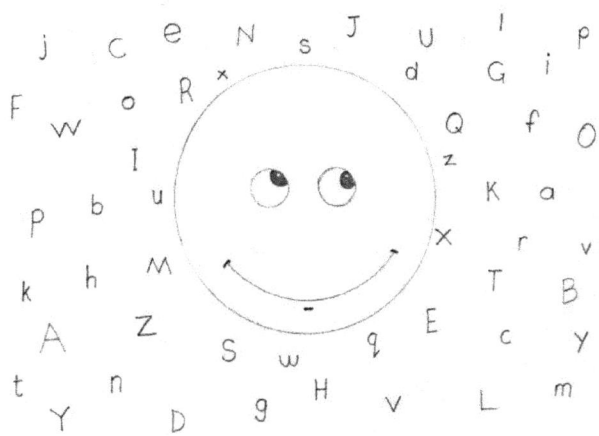

WORDS ARE NOT ENOUGH ©

WORDS ARE NOT ENOUGH

Words are not enough
Alphabets strung in uncertainty
Speech slurred in disbelief
Love endlessly professed
Lacking in action or substance
Intentions of the heart
Inexpressible by vocabulary
Pledges frustrated by timelines
Lofty dreams built with bricks of vapour
Visions written on sand
Children of promise orphaned by unfulfilment
In foster care of compromise
Doubt takes up tenancy
Sin, its landlord

Grace grants clemency
Faith offers a new lease
Adopted by rectitude
Shut doors avert imminent destruction
Redirecting the path to destiny
Visions conceptualized begin to materialize
Pipe dreams turn reality
Old debts reconciled
The hearts intent
Superseded by divine counsel
Love endures its rule
Substantiated by fidelity
After all said and undone
Words alone are not enough